IT CAN

Happen

TO YOU TOO

BELIEVE IT

By

Janet Striverson

Dedication

I would like to dedicate and thank God that he has allowed me to write this book and tell and share my story to help others.

I really could not have written it without his help. To my daughter Candyce and my son Jason who really stood by me and encouraged me along the way to tell my story. I dedicate this book to my family who has always been my support system. No matter what they have always believed in me. I also dedicate this book to all the families that have lost a child or children in tragedy. Those that are still grieving over the loss of their loved ones. Most of all I dedicate this book to my precious daughter, my first born, Janell who lives in my heart. I will never forget you and I know someday I will see you again. I will love you forever.

1980 - 1983

Introduction

I thank God that he has always given us the right to make the right choices in life. But we can also choose to make the wrong choices in life. Whichever one I choose, the choice still is mine. We can make a bad choice which becomes a mistake. A mistake is something we regret doing. The worst thing is to continue to make the same mistake. It can cause you grief, sorrow, and pain for life. We must all think before we run across a busy street without making sure that the road is clear both ways. Especially when we are being distracted along the way. Stop, look, and listen to the warning signs. A mistake can turn to regret. Regrets can cause you a lifetime of pain deep down in your heart and soul. "Listen" Take your time in life! "What is your hurry".

I was born and raised in Indiana. Both of my parents were in the household. They made sure we had everything that we needed. I come from a home of ten boys and three girls. My father was a hard-working construction worker, and my mother was a cook at a local facility at a state hospital. After a while, my father and his best friend had their own construction business for a while, and they still held onto their current job. My father was also a hunter, and he loved the sport. My father also loved to fish. Of course, I was the designated child to whom he would bring the bucket of fish so that I could clean them. I learned so much from my father. And at most times he would start the barbeque grill on the front porch, and he would leave me to watch it while he went somewhere. That is how I learned to barbecue so well was from my dad. I would burn it until I perfected it. He was such a good cook. He would come home from work on snow or rainy days. Because he could not work construction when it was wet. So he would always cook something good for us. And the neighborhood kids would hang around to eat. My father fed just about everybody in the neighborhood. We went to church every Sunday. He always told us, "We would get a star in our crown depending on how many kids we rounded up for Sunday school. Some of those same kids are saved Christians today. My Mother and my Father were Soul winners.

Now, I am not going to leave my mother out of the kitchen. She was the main cook. She would make homemade sweet rolls and homemade biscuits. She even made homemade syrup for us because there were so many of us. I can remember on Sunday morning, we had to get up early in the morning. My father and my mom would fix fried bologna in gravy, along with rice and biscuits. They always had the Pastor and his wife over for dinner on Sundays. I remember them always making homemade vanilla ice cream for dessert. Of course, my mother made pound cakes, tea cakes, peanut butter cookies, etc., during the holidays. Now, my father's specialty was banana pudding. He even made them for people in the neighborhood. Enough talking about food. But that's the kind of childhood that I grew up in. I am smiling as I type this because we had a lot of good times. I remember believing in Santa Claus until I was about twelve or thirteen until I saw my father and older brothers bringing bikes and toys out of the trunk of his car on Christmas Eve. I can remember trick or treating until I was seventeen years old. Oh, by the way, my mother made the best peanut brittle, too. I wouldn't want to leave that out of my book. One reason is that she would break it up and give us grown kids bags until she passed away. We were grown and had our own kids.

I started writing songs and poetry when I was fourteen years old. I regret not playing the piano and organ like I was supposed to. Because later on, through the years, God gifted me to put melodies and lyrics to my songs. I remember when my mother bought my first little piano, and I took lessons in school. But I lost interest. I regret that I did not take the time to do so. Because now I have to pay people to play for me. I said that to say this: whatever God has assigned you to do, Do It. Do the full course. You never know what parents see in you. Or even someone else. We all have a purpose in life. We were created for God's purpose. And you never know where it will take you in life.

The Story

Sometimes, we get sidetracked in life, and we venture off into our own way. We stray away or become distracted along the way. You know, when I was growing up. I was taught by my parents and society to get an education, go to college, and then get married in that order. If you were not married by the time you were twenty-one or 25, everyone thought something was wrong with you. It seemed like people respected you more if you were married or went to college. Yes, indeed, make your parents and family proud. Now, I don't want you to think I was Miss- goody two shoes. But there were some things that I just proposed not to do. I took a home study course in computer programming at home first. I knew I wanted to go to college. And I knew I wanted to leave home and someday move to another city. So, that being said, off to college. The name of the school at that time was AMTC, Automation Machine Training Center.

So, I graduated from high school and college. I got my diploma in computer programming. I came home instead of trying to stay in Kansas. I had no job or money, so I came home. Bored as I don't know what. I had to find a job. I moved in with my sister. Now, the reason I moved in with her when I came back home was because I told my parents that I wasn't coming back home. Guess what? They changed my bedroom into another room. That's why I moved in with my oldest sister. I remember telling them that I would not be returning home after I graduated. I told them that I would live in Kansas City. They sure showed me some tough love. They made sure that room was taken when I got back home. I got my first job as a teacher's aide at a local middle school. Actually it was my old junior high school. I soon found a better job working for a big moving company. It was and still is standing today. I copied contracts from four p.m. until 12 a.m. in the morning. And that is how I met my husband. I met him on the job, because he would give me a ride home from work. My brother would give me a ride there. Or I would ride the bus there.

Later on I regretted that I didn't continue to ride the bus. Anyway, we started dating, and I got engaged on February fourteen, 1977, and we were married on June twenty-fifth, 1977. It was such a beautiful wedding. One of the ladies on my job volunteered to make my dress and bouquets, which saved me a lot of money. I had a medium size wedding. This man wined and dined me before and after we were married. He was the love of my life. I thought I was the love of his life also. I could look on my desk and there would be a dozen roses, yellow or red. Sometimes, he would invite some of my coworkers to lunch. He was the one who made me start wearing make-up and false eyelashes. I thought you would like to know that. He would take me shopping at boutiques and the mall. And he would pick out all my clothes. He would make sure my hair was right. He even told me how to wear my hair. I was such a plain Jane at first. Until he made me who he wanted me to be. This is a good point to make right here. Don't let anyone make you into who they want you to be. I could not drive a car. Matter of fact, it was he who taught me to drive at twenty-three years old. Only because I would fuss so badly about how he would leave me alone in our apartment while he went out with friends.

I did not even look like myself anymore. And by the way, he was my first, if you know what I mean. So, I did not know what to do without him. Isn't that something.? Now, before I got married, I went to school. My mother, my brother, and his wife drove me all the way to Kansas. Twelve hours from home, and I lived in a dorm with strangers who I did not know. But I lost my independence when I married this man. I was so used to being with him all the time. We worked together. We went out together. Not to mention, we were best friends. I could not dance a lick. But we went dancing because he was a good dancer. I did my best to keep up with him. All this was at the beginning of our marriage. Oh, how we gossiped about other married couples and said we would never be that way. He always liked nice things and was very materialistic. We were always living above our means. But we had good jobs, but did not know how to manage money. He loved to entertain guests and have parties at our house. I was still trying to adapt to this new life. I could not keep up with the bills by myself. I would give him the money, only to find out he was not paying the bills. I trusted him with the money.

We could not even pay our bills. But we could go out and party and have fun all the time. We started to spiral toward Poverty, and love went out. We started fussing and arguing about every little thing. We started not to get along with each other. He started spending more time with friends than me. Any way he could find a way to leave me by myself, he did it. He stopped inviting me to places. So, one day, I said to him, "Maybe we should have a baby." Surely, I thought it would make our marriage better. WRONG. So, I got pregnant and began to threaten a miscarriage. I had to quit my job and stay off my feet. Because I started to hemorrhage.

My husband started to complain about his job. And guess what? He quit his job also. So there we were both with no job. Arguing all the time because there was no money coming in. The car got repossessed. We left to go for a walk one day and left boiling eggs on the stove. Someone reported they smelled smoke coming from our apartment. The fire department had to break in to put out the fire. We got evicted and had to move. Mind you, I am pregnant at this time. I am threatening a miscarriage, and we moved and did not have a bed to sleep in. So, my only option was to sleep in a chair. My ex-husband's aunt was nice enough to let us live in one of her rentals.

Our beautiful daughter Janell C was born on February 25, 1980. Our bundle of joy she was. I went back to work after my six weeks were up. My job rehired me, thank God. My husband got a new job, which he hated. He complained so much he quit. He got another job and pretended to be going to work. Only to find out that he was fired. With one income and a new baby, we could hardly make it. Every time we argued, he would threaten to leave me. He wanted me to put up with his mess and not say a word. Finally, he told me he wanted to be carefree. He said that if I did not leave, he would leave me anyway. He began stealing money from me and writing bad checks. Eventually, I left, Janell and I. I told him that I could do bad by myself. And believe me, that is just what I did.

I wanted to fix things and prove that I was not a failure. When you are hurting and being tossed to and from all over the place! You do not see clearly and you sure aren't thinking straight. I was doing fine, me and my little Janell.

. Why drag her into this torment of life? She didn't ask to come here. I invited her into my tragic life of loss, lust, and failure. This was all my doing. I went back to paying attention to God. And along the way I met the devil face to face. 'People, I tell you the truth". Don't allow yourself to get sidetracked along the way to progress and healing. It can happen so easily. You can be tricked. You think it is a new beginning, and it can end up being a disaster.

Janell and I moved into a two-bedroom town house, very nice. We were very happy. We were safe, secured and content. It is a good thing to wait on God in the midst of your troubles, heartaches and disappointments.

It is a sad thing to move into Satan's territory. I was devastated and hurt. There were people telling me I needed somebody also. Get you a man. Listen, stop listening to every person. I don't care if it is family. You get as close to God as you can. If you have to walk alone, then so be it.

Do you know there are some people who want you to fail? It didn't seem real that I was only married for four years. I was left alone wandering around in the wilderness. Please don't misunderstand me. The choices that were made were still mine. If you choose to go the wrong way, you will suffer in the end.

Trying to find my baby's father was like pulling teeth. I could not find him to help with anything. I needed things for our daughter. I was still trying to find this new way of life, being single again. My point is that you stay with God if you have him in your life. If you don't stay by yourself, especially if you have children. Keep going, moving forward. My ex-husband wanted to be friends. How do you remain friends with someone that you love and want to spend your life with? Someone who broke my heart and promised to take care of me. I wished for me anyway that we could mend our relationship. He never wanted marriage again, he said or a child. Wow. "I'll never have a child again," is what he said to me. Many times, I prayed that God would heal our marriage, and it never happened. There were other things that blocked him from wanting me. I found that out later.

I mentioned earlier that I backslide from God. You can want something so bad, but you still have to face what's real. I had to learn the hard way through many disappointments and heartaches. I don't want no one that doesn't want me. Let it go. Learn how to be by yourself. I had never shacked before in my life. I would never do such a thing. That's what I said. My husband and I promised we would never divorce. We would always be together. We used to gossip about everyone we knew that was having problems in their marriage. (Not us, NO NO NO). That will never happen to us. So we said and thought. My husband was my first and last. So I thought we were in love, so I thought. What happened to the dances and dinners we went to on Friday night? What happened tonight talks, day talks, going for walks in the neighborhood, waking up to roses, dieting together, best friends. Our marriage was dissolved in May of 1982. My ex never showed up for the finalizing of the divorce, so the judge did it without him. I sent the papers to his mother's address, and that was it. I had no forwarding address for him. I was introduced to a man, along with Satan assigned to take me out and my daughter out. He had nothing, no money. He had unemployment that he used for his needs only. This man was worse than my ex-husband. He drank beer and got high all day when he got his money. And when he did not have it. He was another person, sad, mad, depressed, and ugly. Like I said, I met him through my sister, a big mistake. A few months later, I let him move in with me. My home of contentment became a disaster. I jumped out of the pan and landed in the fire.

Whenever he was gone from my house, it was so peaceful. No fussing, no trying to figure out how to make him happy. "If you leave me, I will kill myself," he would threaten every day. I knew I did not want him anymore. I think he knew that, too. His mother told me not to leave my daughter alone with him. I did not know why, he seemed ok to me, after all I was just going to the store! I did it a few times. Why didn't she tell me why? And why didn't I listen? One of the mothers at the church that I backslide from told me, "Whatever you do, do not put no man over your child. " Listen, not only did I put him over her, I was going to marry him! We got engaged, we had picked out rings and put a down payment on them. I was going to show my ex-husband that I could get married again. After all, it was a family member of mine that told me, Janell and I didn't look good all alone without a man. After my sister introduced me to him. Not blaming anybody, but listening to people when you are trying to find your way never works. My sister called me to tell me of some things she had heard about this man, of a child that had been abused and died while he was watching her. I said, "OK, I will be careful." A friend of mine told me about the rumor. I didn't pay any attention to that. I thought I finally found someone who wanted me. You see, it was all about me getting my needs met. I thought I had a future husband for me and a father for Janell.

Then I really got comfortable and started dropping Janell and the stranger off at his mother's house. So I thought. I am not sure to this day that he took her there because I would pull off and go on to work. The police questioned me, and detectives asked me if she had ever been in the hospital. I said no. Before this, I had started to trust this stranger man more and more with Janell. When we would go to our family gatherings he always kept her close to him. As if he really love her. We would go to his mother's apartment sometimes and they acted like they really loved us. Nothing made sense. When I came home one day, I found my beautiful daughter, my angel beaten severely, sitting on this man's lap, and he was combing her hair. My daughter could not stand up. I had to stand her up like a puppet on a string, and she was limp. The first thing he said to me when I walked into the door. "You better get her to a hospital," he yelled at me. "She has been throwing up all day. I took her from his arms, and she was so stiff. I took her into the bedroom and took all her clothes off. I saw no bruises. There was a very small one on her cheek. I picked her up, took her to his mother, and asked her what he did to my baby. She made up something to the fact that maybe she had a disease. I shouted, "What did he do to my child"? I went and got my sister to take me to the nearest hospital because I did not know the way. Especially at that time, I knew something was terribly wrong with my little two-year-old, who would soon be turning three the next month. I walked into the hospital and told the emergency vet that I had left my little girl while I went to work with this man. And then I came home to find her sitting on his lap while he was combing her hair. Because I was starting to remember the rumors that I had heard. Everything that happened to the other child was under suspicion.

Neither the police nor detectives could find anything at first. They kept questioning me all night. Janell slipped into a coma. Finally, another detective came back to me and asked me again what he was doing with Janell when I got home. I said he had her on his lap, putting her hair in a ponytail. The detective, with the other ones, nurses, and police were trying to figure out what happened. The detectives called me into her room and showed and gave me the bad news. She had contusions and severe brain damage. When they finally looked at her scalp with a flashlight and found all the injuries. They called his mother's house to speak to him. Because that is where he was. He had run on foot to his mother's house for her to cover up for him. She told the police that he was asleep. The police arrested him, and he confessed to beating my child with a closed fist until she passed out. When she came to, he beat her repeatedly over the head with his fist again. He confessed to murdering a four-month-old boy that was left in his care, another two-year-old left in his care, and another child that he had beaten so severely that he is in special needs care to this day and now was about to kill my Janell. I kept telling my baby how sorry I was that I allowed this to happen to her. My Janell had fluid on her brain also. So, they had to drill a hole in her head to drain the fluid off. She stayed in the coma for two weeks. When she came out of it. It looked like there was hope. She began to notice pictures of Mickey Mouse that she had at home. She was pointing at things she remembered. She was learning to kick a ball. She was in a wheelchair. They took her from me and turned her over to the state. They said when she comes home, she can never be around this man again, or they would take her from me for good. I agreed, thinking she was coming home with me. She was in the hospital for a month. And then things turned for the worse one day while she was there. She had so many seizures, one right after another. She was given all kinds of medicine. Day by day, I watched as my little girl was fading away from me. I got to spend time with her, holding her in my arms, and I kept apologizing to her. The detectives had his confession on tape and asked me if I wanted to see it. I told them no.

It was my suggestion to take her to Riley, Indianapolis Children's Hospital, in the hope that they could save her. On my wish, they took us both to Riley Hospital. My Janell was breathing so hard as if it was her last breath. Her trach began to close up. By the time we got to Riley, she was worse. I believe they all knew back home she was going to die. But they let me take her to Riley anyway. I had to tell them what happened to my daughter. I have to tell them that my so-called boyfriend did this terrible thing to my Janell. The nurses made me leave the room. I sat in the cafeteria reading a book that someone gave me from work. It was called 'When bad things happen to good people.' As I was trying to concentrate on something in the book that would help, I heard a voice say, "The will of God." Soon afterward, a nurse came to tell me that Janell had stopped breathing. They asked me if I would like to see her. Of course, I wanted to see my baby girl. When I got to her room, she was lying there so peaceful. No more harsh breathing, no more flesh falling from her bones as if she had been in a fire. Medication, the drilling hole in her head to drain the fluids off had disappeared. A chaplain came to talk with me. She asked me if I knew where Janell went. I told her, "Yes, that her spirit went back to God." I told her that I would see her again. The power of God kept holding me up. The man who murdered my daughter only got twenty-five years. He got nothing for the other children. Because, at the time, the statute of limitations was ten years. We all trusted this man with our children. The social workers told me later that he was bipolar. I saw nothing and no signs because I didn't know what to look for. He was out in twelve years.

I could not see because I was hurting. He smiled at her as if he cared. But he always kept her close to him. That is how the enemy keeps his prey right where he can control their every move. Pretending like he cared and loved her. Really his mother could have told me that he had a problem with children. They moved from another state, knowing that this man had beaten a child, that is Special needs to this day. Knowing that he beat another baby till it pounced off the couch, closed fist dead, four months old, a little girl beaten till dead, of put-on record as suspension. And, of course, now my Janell. They asked him why he didn't tell me that he could not be left alone with children. He said he did not want to lose me. Wow. What a kick in the stomach and slap in the face. I remember, at one point, he told me that he would take something to his grave. But he never said what it was. He had a tattoo that read Osmosis on his hand.

Concealed: Osmosis. When I asked him who osmosis was. He told me, "You don't want to meet him. He is a bad MF." In my mind, I thought he was talking about someone he drank with or knew. That was the other side of him he was so proud of that it came out in his actions to hurt children or people. He was suicidal, alright enough, but not to hurt himself but Others. I want you to take notes of what I am saying as I write this book. Some of these are signs that you look for or see.

Pay Attention: Pay attention to how close they keep their prey to them.

How they Lie: He told me one day when I left her with him that the pot pie was too hot and burned her arm a little. "Liar," now I know he did that to her.

I'll Kill myself: If a person tells you, "If you leave them, they will kill themselves." Most likely, they will kill you or someone that you love so hard.

Coward: Cowards hurt children. Children and babies cannot defend themselves.

Lame excuse: They said in court that his father beat him and his mother. And at the age of sixteen, he ran away.

Help: Help is available for anyone who wants help. His mother could have gotten him help or at least warned people. When you move from another state no one knows you really. "Parents do not hide if your child has problems while growing up. And then you move away, and others die because of what you could have warned or told them. Tell them why they can't be around children. "Please," don't give them a hint and not tell them why! That person can run or get out of the situation.

This man was full of Demons that were assigned to kill children. The only reason he confessed was because I told them he did something to her. And I also told them to ask about the other children that people told me about, and then he told the detectives how he did it.

Phyco-Path: He had the nerve to write me a letter wishing me Happy Mother's Day. It had a big heart drawn and him expressing his love for me. And how I was his soul mate. And how our hearts burned for one another. He even told me that we would always be together. He never once mentioned my daughter. The letter came through my mail on my Job. I gave it to the detectives. They threatened to add more charges if he did it again. And by the way, this man looked at me in court, rolling his eyes at me while in court as if it was my fault. How long would he have kept murdering Babies? That is what he thought he would take to his grave. Now, I am telling you this to be aware of Wolves dressed in Sheep's Clothing. My daughter turned three years old the next month. She spent her time in the hospital on her birthday, February 25, and she passed away on March the fifth, 1983.

You know, when Janell was in intensive care for children, there was a lady there with her baby, and she and Janell shared a room. The child's mother was a Christian, and she would try to encourage me while we lived at the hospital for a month. She would walk around me every day and quote this scripture. Romans 8:28. And we know that all things work together for good, to them that love God, to them who are called, according to his purpose. I would say to myself, you call this good? My baby's flesh is melting like fire and she was doing so good at first. And now she is dying. You call this good? She was right!

I was a Christian that was backslidden. One that was hurting so bad that she could not see the forest due to the trees that were in the way. I had fallen from grace and made all kinds of mistakes, one after the other. Trying to do things my way, trying to prove a point. Young and old ladies, you can make it. My prayer is that you read my book and know that there is a God in heaven. Our heavenly Father, who can sustain us. No matter what we go through. If you have not, give your heart to Jesus Christ and never stray away from him. Go to God when people abandon you. The first thing we want to do is go and get another man so that he can hurt us more because we have not been healed. Satan is waiting to take you out. This man threatened me one time while we were arguing that he would do something to make me never trust a man again. I had no clue what he was talking about. He never hit me, but he was taking it out on my baby. He was charged with involuntary manslaughter. He received a sentence of twenty-five years. I repeat again that he only served twelve years.

Please don't listen to people who persuade you to get another man. Wait on God because you are in a lot of pain right then. Especially not listening to some family members. Some will tell you to go and get a man because you are still young. They have no idea what God is going to do with you, and you don't either. The plan of God is Greater. Jeremiah 29:11 "For I know the plans I have for you," declares the Lord, "Plans to prosper you and not to harm you. Plans to give you hope and a future. God has a purpose and a plan for you and me.

I am here to warn women not to put men over their children. God will give you the power to wait on what he has for you. Sometimes, we marry the wrong people because we don't wait. We are just so in love with the devil. It only takes one person to cost you a lifetime. I chose not to let them. They are the ones that had the problem. But still, I chose them. When a man tells you who he is, someone shows you who they are. Believe them. And don't think it can't happen to you. I graduated, went to college, had a good job, and was taking care of me and Janell, but I thought I could not do without a man. Yes, I said it. I was looking for love in all the wrong places.

Revenge: revenge got me in trouble, trying to get back at my ex-husband. How many have tried besides me to get even and pick something worse than what you had? That is another chapter in my life. But my aim and mission is to help others. Go on and humble yourselves and do the right thing. I hope you know that there are some people who will lead you the wrong way, control you, because you trust their judgment. They still have their children. Some of them are deceased now, and you are still left here to go on. Think about it. Satan doesn't care who he uses to try to destroy you. By the grace of God, you can rise up again.

I had to give away all her Christmas toys and toys all together with other things. I suffered for years. If I can cause you not to go through the pain that I went through, then this book is worth writing. The trauma that I went through has taken me years to heal. But God is my healer, and he has kept me. At one time, I was suicidal after Janell died. Life is worth living because Jesus lives. And I know I will see Janell again. What did I have to live for? I had no child, low self-esteem, bitterness, anxiety, claustrophobic hatred.... the list went on and on.

Notice I said Went. It was God that healed me and still is doing a mighty work in my life. If this has happened to you or similar, there is available help. I am so glad that Jesus bore the shame so I would not have to. Some things happen to keep you from your purpose. Some things are mistakes. You didn't mean to, but it happened. And it could happen to you too if you are not careful. I want to talk to you about how not to think that every man that you meet is your husband. That's what got me into trouble. After my failed marriage, do you know I still wanted a husband? We need to wait. Some of us have never waited for anything in life. We mess our lives up and the lives of others. Because in the midst of it all, I hurt my family. My friends were hurt and disappointed. And also the people who warned me were disappointed that I disobeyed when they were sent to warn me. Warning always comes before destruction. I am a living testimony that God can give you a second chance to stay with him and to also be content loving God. I have two more children, a son and a daughter, who are all grown up now. I have a thirty-eight-year-old son and a thirty-nine-year-old daughter. Now, at one point in my life. I had to tell my children about what happened to their sister. I believe they were eight and nine years old. Their response was very heart-breaking and touching. You must understand that at that time, Janell was my only child. And no mother wants to bury their child. Who in the world would want their child to leave here before them?

I do recommend seeing if the person you are leaving your child with has a problem with children crying. Because this man told the detectives that Janell would not stop crying. And I know she was crying when I went off to work that morning. I also had to give her puppy away. I wish that the puppy could talk that day. My brother lived right up the stairs from us and did not hear anything that morning. The detective asked him why he didn't knock on my brother's door and took her to him. Better yet, they wanted to know why he didn't just leave her there. Now, remember he had a friend he called Osmosis engraved on his hand. And he was also suicidal! In my opinion, whatever caused this Demon to rise up in him to murder children was created inside of him, and his mother covered it up and never got him the professional help he needed. Running to another state did not help. Three of us women are left without our children and one child in special care because of this one man. He never confessed any of this until after my baby Janell died. He must have enjoyed what he was doing because he tattooed the name on his hand. And when I asked him about who it was, he had a smile on his face when he said, "You don't want to mess with him. He is a bad blank blank...and he is dangerous." That is what he said to me. Remember, he said that he knew something and that he would never tell anyone. And that he would take it to his grave. So, he never intended to get help.

My Daughter, who was two at the time, another little girl who was two at the time, and a four-month-old baby boy all died in the same city. He tried to say Janell fell off the bed. I told them at the hospital that she did not. Because deep down in my heart, I knew he had done something to my little girl. The bed wasn't even four feet high, I told them. Then they thought that he threw her against a wall because her spleen was messed up. But when they put that flashlight through her hair, that is what proved it. The other little girl, he said she fell down the stairs trying to follow him to the mailbox. "Liar". He got away with it, all put under suspicion of a blunt object. If parents do not speak up and push it and say that they know something happened whether you heard rumors or not. One person moved far away after her son was killed by this man. It was swept under the rug. Then, when it happened to Janell, he started confessing. 'And be sure your sin will find you out,' numbers 32:23. Some way and somehow, God will reveal things. He is our Vindicator. Don't sweep anything under the rug or run and feel guilty that you left them there with the babysitter. This thinking is a problem. If they are yelling at your children, most likely, they will mistreat them when you are not around. They will also harm them. Going to the police can save another child's life. Had it been known for sure he was doing this by someone, Janell would be here today. I imagine that they didn't believe it or did not care. Especially if you can walk away and do nothing. Or maybe you don't want to believe it. This man stayed depressed. It is OK to tell someone that you cannot be left with children alone. This will give you a chance to take your children and run.... fast as you can, get away from them. If not, you are going to forget about what you were warned about or felt, and you will leave them alone with your children. I hope you know that a person can gain your trust by looking so sincere and pretending that they love you and your children. And all the time, they have a killer instinct to use your children as prey.

Help the Police to catch a predator. The detectives, police, and the hospital staff. They told me later that they knew that I had nothing to do with it. Because of the way that I said he did something to her, and that I was trying to find out what he had done to her while I was at work. It happened at eleven o'clock that morning on a Friday. I called him at eleven 'o'clock that morning to check on Janell, and I asked if everything was ok. He assured me that everything was fine. I felt the need to go home at lunch, and I did not. I had this feeling inside of me that something was wrong. I suppose he made bail, and the police took him to my apartment to get his belongings. I never saw him again until I went to court in another town. He only did 12 years. I have never seen him again. This happened forty years ago. Please save a child or children's life. If you see abuse, it is important that you report it. Even if you suspect abuse, report it. If it is just a rumor, report it. If you feel trapped by a man or a person and you feel that there is no way out. Get help; tell someone that you feel threatened. Especially when you feel something is wrong and you are afraid to leave. You may feel like I did, that after a while, you really did not want to be around that person. Once you have seen they had nothing to offer. If this has happened to you, get counseling. I talked to one Pastor who tried to help me. But at the time, what he said made no sense to me. He was right, but at that time, it made no sense to me. Later on, it made sense. And he was right. God healed me through it all. He healed me through his word and his forgiveness. It has taken me a long time to heal. I believe more counseling would have helped instead of walking around bitter and hurt. At that time, I did not think I needed all that counseling and therapy. I did need it, but I was too stubborn and high-minded to get it. "It is available to you, take it." Even with me, just putting Janell and my story into words has helped and healed a lot of areas in my life. I needed to get it out so that I could help someone else before it happens to them and to know that it is not their fault. They are the ones who have problems and refuse to get help. They think that they do not have a problem, and they continue to hurt children. Hurting people hurt people. They are very selfish and do not want to get help when help is available. I am a born-again Christian, a licensed Missionary, Evangelist, and Teacher of the word of God that spreads the good news of Jesus Christ wherever I go. I am single and I learned to wait on God. I love to sit down in my kitchen with young women or wherever God allows it to be and share my story. I tell them that they can make it without a man. I let them know that those were mistakes that they made, and that God forgives, and that they can start all over again with the help of God. Someone told me that I would minister to women just like me and help them. I was so bitter at the time and told them that I hoped no one does to them what was done to me. Yes, it is happening even as I write this book. And I think to myself if they don't listen to me! Maybe they will read my book and refer to it as they go about life. Or maybe they will think about what happened to me.

As women and young ladies, we have to stop listening to society. I will go as far as to say stop listening to other people also. Sometimes, there are people who don't want to see you make it. And most of the time they are not going anywhere themselves. Remember, misery loves company. I myself had to find my own identity all over again. There were things I had to go through for years that affected me. You see, there is an aftermath or leftover debris in your life when you go through tragedy. My first identity was lost when I met my ex-husband, who began to change me. I had so much make-up on until I did not know anymore who I was... So many people have an identity crisis, and they are messed up because they get involved with someone who is already messed up. People can spot your insecurities and vulnerabilities right away. Then sometimes, we want to prove to the people when you are alone for a certain amount of time, that there is nothing wrong with you. So, people start looking at you differently, and you start thinking the same thing.

Please don't react to others' opinions about you. After all of this I still wanted to be married again. I had to get away from that and wait. If you don't take your time, it will cost you something. I was surrounded by people that wanted to get married so badly. I was one of them also. So, I separated myself from them. Some got married, and I was still asking God when my turn would come again. Well, I am still single, but I am stronger and I don't spend my time thinking about a man and being married. I love the Lord with all that is within me. I wake up thinking of Jesus and go to sleep thinking of Jesus. Throughout the day my mind is on Jesus. I think about the things he wants me to do in ministry. How can I minister to young people and help them not to do what I did? I had to get away from people who were carnal-minded all of the time.

Like I said, some of them got married. And some got married, and the husband died after a couple of years. And some of the women died before the men. So they didn't even get to enjoy them for a long time.

I am just saying that sometimes God wants to use you before you get married. Maybe you won't do it if you get married. Because you will have to do the things that please your husband. Maybe you won't be able to jump out of bed and pray. Maybe you won't be able to study like you should. Unless he is saved and on fire for God like you are. But to live in Christ is a great gain. Why do we always want the cart before the horse? God has work for us to do. What is so beautiful is when God gives you a saved husband because you waited. He rewards us openly because we remain faithful to him. I give myself away so that God can use me. I am sold out. Of course, I think of what it would be like to have a saved mate in my life. But not like I used to and being desperate. Being desperate and thirsty is what gets us in trouble. Can I get an Amen? Being disobedient gets us in trouble. When we have been counseled to wait, we go ahead of God. Then our children suffer, and we suffer. I have tried many times in my flesh to go ahead of God. And I have made mistakes along the way. I have two more children and still no husband. I have been engaged four times since then. But I refused to marry them. Another thing I would like to mention in my book is that do not marry a man in prison. Please do not get involved with a man in prison. Wait to see what he will be like when he gets out of prison.

He can do right while he is in prison, and most likely, he is looking for a place to stay. Ask me how I know. My Pastor and wife counseled me through the whole thing. I am running down there with a sister in the Lord to see her husband. She stuck with me long enough until her husband got out of prison. Then, I was left hanging to deal with his friend. I was engaged to him. He wanted me to marry him while he was in prison. I was told not to do it and to wait, so I did. He was furious and very angry with me. So he married another young lady who he beat on. I am so glad I didn't do it. They are divorced now. He would take her car and ride other women around in it. I told her not to marry him, and she did it anyway. I had an engagement ring, and so did she. I was told by a Pastor to give it back, and I did.

As a matter of fact, I was told that if I had anything of his, including gifts from him to give them back to him. That way, he would have no reason to come back or break in. That's why he went to prison. Armed Robbery and drugs. That person also molested her daughter, and for a while, they did not get along. She tried to tell her mother. You see, these are all the reasons that we should wait.

Moreover, some of the dating sites are also dangerous. Young women are being murdered. No one ever hears from them again after one date sometimes. My so-called friend introduced me to the man in prison. She and another so-called friend laughed at me. I was so hurt that it did not work out. That man made me so many promises while he was in prison. And he hated me for not marrying him while he was there. Those letters and homemade gifts that they give you while they are in prison. Someone writes the letters and makes those wooden plaques and little wells, etc. I am glad to this day that I did not marry him. You know! You can want something so bad that it seems so real to you that you are convinced that it is so and that it should be. Don't fool yourself. Ask God for wisdom and know how to discern when something is real or not. Sometimes, we do not want to accept the fact that there is always going to be a war going on between the flesh and the spirit. The flesh wants to take over every time.

The strong deliverer will win. You are going to have to hear and listen to someone. Sometimes, God sends people to warn you, like he did me. But sometimes we want to pick and choose our own way. Whether you are saved or not, God loves us. He knows what is best for us. If God can use a donkey to get his point across. Then, he can choose to use whatever and whomever he wants at any time. I want to talk about distractions in life. Things that are put in front of you to keep you from seeing clearly. Remember, I was doing just fine, Janell and I. And this man told my sister, "Here I am." See how the devil can rise up in anybody to destroy you or take you out.

Back in the 80's the statute of limitations was 10 years. They could do nothing about the other children. But now predators are getting more time for killing children than back then. No longer is it being swept under the rug. Someone has got to love children enough to fight and become an advocate for them. We have to stop believing in the baby-sitter. Or that low-down teacher who preys upon the child who doesn't get enough attention at home. Or the child who we leave for someone else to mentor. You know, that one who we leave our children for them to take up time with. Then, later on, through the years, the child tells his or her story. And you never know until they tell it when they get to be a grown-up. We are so busy sometimes working or trying to fulfill a life of our own that we don't see it until it is too late. And we wonder why our children hate us for not protecting them. And sometimes we don't believe them when they are telling us the truth. It took me ten years to forgive and ten yours to heal. I believe that some counseling would have helped. But at that time, I thought no one could help me. And because of the guilt and shame, I did not get any help. All through the years, God has healed and helped me. I am talking about professional help.

My other two children that I had later on in life, I was afraid to leave them with a baby-sitter. I lost so many babysitters and friends that I was accusing them of things that they did not do. There were some that tried to test me because of what happened to me. I let them go. Every year my children turned three, I would take a deep breath. I would think something was going to happen to them. God healed me of that also. So many things had to be restored and replenished in my life. That is why the bible tells us in Psalm 23: 3, 'He restoreth my soul.' Because there are some things that happen in life that will hurt you and wound your very soul. They can hurt you to the core. And there are some repairs that need to be done so that we don't go around hurting other people. Hebrews 12: 15, "Looking diligently lest any man fail of the grace of God, lest any root of bitterness springing up trouble you, and thereby many be defiled." You may not intend to hurt anyone! But if you do not heal, you will. Many people do many things to cover up their hurts and disappointments. Some examples are self-medicating, drinking, getting high off drugs and other substances. The best remedy is to go to God for help. And please go and get counseling. Everyone needs someone to talk to. I would use my friends as a sounding board when I lost my beautiful little girl. As soon as I could, I would dump my life on someone else. Or I wondered if they knew who I was. And no matter how long it has been, you will carry some kind of guilt if you do not develop a close relationship with God. You have to believe that he has forgiven you. And please forgive yourself. I was always playing over and over in my mind. If I had not gone to work that day. If I would have heed to her cry when I went out the door. I trusted this man totally with my baby. And then afterward, and over the years, you see all the red flags. You see all the warning signs that God was showing you. As God begins to strengthen you and you stay in the word of God, you gain the power to overcome.

Power to see clearly. You began to see the plan of God for your life. Stop walking into Satan's traps. The warning signs are there. They were always there. You could not see them because of the hurt and pain that you were going through. Sometimes, you get introduced by Satan to other people who corrupt good manners. I Corinthians 15:33 says Be not deceived: evil communications corrupt good manners. You can be the best that you can be. Satan can send someone to your weakest point in your life, and their assignment is to try to destroy you. Yes, you can come from a good Christian home and still miss God. You can leave his divine protection for you and your family to go stepping into his territory and mess up. You cannot trust everyone. Everyone is not as good of a person as you think. You are going through something, and they are going through something. You got bad nerves because of what you are going through. And you did not know at the time that they were bipolar, mentally ill, unstable, schizophrenia, and a serial killer of babies and little children. Until they get his or her history after the fact. Or they move to another state and keep the secret with the family. Whatever you do in the dark! It will come to light. If you cannot stand to hear noises like a child crying, please get some help. Or you will have more problems later on in life. Some people are just hateful and mean-spirited in life. Some people don't like nobody. Some don't even love themselves. The world is made up of all kinds of people. The good, the bad, and the ugly. Ask God to give you discernment in life. It can prevent you from a lot of pain.

Another subject I would like to mention in my book is: The phrase "Something told me! Who do you believe that was? Or I should have listened to those who tried to warn me of this person. Because we never think it can happen to us. What about that gut feeling you get when you went left and you should have gone right? Or you were told to wait on God, and you went ahead of him anyway, and then you blamed God. "God, why did you allow this to happen? When you feel like you can do bad by yourself. You sometimes do just bad. When you won't hear no one but yourself. You are headed for trouble. Everybody does not mean you well. Look, listen, and pray. God hears a sinner's prayer when he or she is repenting, or crying to God to get them out. Sometimes, this man would leave, and I would let him right back in. I promised God that I would not take him back that final time. Because I realized the peace that I had when he was not around. I did not keep my promise to God. If you keep playing with fire, you will get burnt.

If you are going through a situation. And you have children, and you need some time to think. If you do not have friends to watch them. There are shelters that will watch your children for you in some states.

Do not leave them with a stranger. When I say that, I am talking about your boyfriend or your new boyfriend. Don't leave them with lazy people who want to sleep all day and do not want to be bothered. Before I retired, I had a coworker tell me on the job that she did not like kids. I looked at her strangely. Because I knew that she had a son who was five years old. She said she never would babysit anyone else's children. She said, "I just don't like kids. She was honest enough to say that. Now, I don't know if she knew what happened to me. But she confessed it to me. Take notice that she told me that she does not babysit other people's children. And she is a very good mother and takes good care of her son. She had sense enough to tell me that she did not like watching kids. Wouldn't it be nice if a whole lot of people would be honest and tell the truth? It sure would save a lot of little lives. Another young lady that was training me for a new job. She had a picture of a beautiful little girl on her desk. She told me it was her daughter and that she did not live with her right now. Due to some boyfriend that shook her baby girl until there was brain damage done.

She told me that she would be getting her back when she went to court. So, I shared my story in the hope that it would put fear in her not to let him come near her or her child. I told her your little girl lived, and mine passed away. I told her how blessed she was to get another chance to raise and protect her. I did not get a second chance at raising my Janell. But it sure taught me a good life lesson. I wanted to die, and I mean die. It was planted in my head to get married again. Whatever you fail in, leave it alone. Don't keep trying to make it happen. You will keep making mistake after mistake. You will keep putting your hand in the fire to be burned. Now don't think I did not meet men after that. None of them worked out. Because I kept making bad choices and not waiting. If you think you can run your own life, you are so wrong. Because we were created for God's purpose. He is the boss. Not you or I making our own way. Sometimes, we keep getting attracted to the same type of man. Attached to that same spirit, and wonder why. I was attracted to men that tricked me. They never abused me physically. When I say that, I mean hit me.

But they abused me in other ways by being deceitful, liars, pretenders, and getting whatever was left inside of me. I asked God after the death of my daughter why did this happen to me. The holy spirit spoke to me and said you never waited for what I had for you. I met other men. How do you think I have two more beautiful children? Still was being tricked. I was engaged to some of them even afterward. I did not marry anyone of them. I was tempted, but I didn't do it. My former pastor and his wife walked me through this one situation. The man that was in prison and I had his ring. When I passed the test and did not marry him. Sometimes, my pastor would put my story in his sermon. He would say, "She did not marry him though." I believe that someone needed it. I would say, "Can I marry him while he is in prison?" He would always tell me to wait and see what he would be like when he got out.

Then, he would ask me at that time how I was going to consummate the marriage. How is he going to take care of you and your children? "Think." Sometimes, we just don't think or see the whole picture. And we just think, "I got this." We don't have nothing, and we are nothing without Christ in our lives. Aren't you tired of the same old same old? Aren't you tired of wondering when Mr. Right will come your way? I am writing this book with the intent that someone will stop in their tracks and stop moving so fast. Impulse is a sudden strong, and ineffective urge or desire to act. That was me. Always doing things on impulse. Compulsive is resulting from or relating to an irresistible urge. "Oh, I need to get married." I was not ready to get married either. I did it on impulse and compulsive behavior. I was young and had a lot of dreams for my music and writing. I was so happy that someone wanted to marry me, and I thought, make me happy. Well, I got news for you. In my opinion, it is what most men and women desire in life. There is a commitment. Just like we make a commitment to obey and love God.

I am just saying this in my case. The closer my walk is with the Lord. My desires have changed in my life. I seek to please him. As a single and saved woman that is what I am supposed to be doing. Not seeking a man. God knows what each and every one of us needs. My Pastor used to tell me, "God is going to give you a husband. I must have been so thirsty at that time. I had to grow and still growing. You think I would not even want a man after what happened to me and my Janell? I still had that urge. God is amazing. He will take our desires and make them his desires. And along the way, you don't know what is in the plan of God. I tell you this. I will never try to get it on my own. Let us use our God-given sense. As we travel this life, we are going to make some mistakes but we do not have to keep making the same ones. I often hear people say that God has given them another chance. He has given me chance after chance. Many chances God has given me. I always become an open book and I am very transparent with others. I don't ever want to give anyone the impression that I got it all together.

I am teachable. What I thought about after and while going through the loss of my Janell. Listen to what I said to people. "Don't understand why this happened to me? I tried one time to shack up with somebody, and look what happened?" That was my plan. But you see, God had another plan and a purpose for me. He had it all the time. But I decided to go my way and let the devil detour and trick me. Don't let Satan put you on another path that can affect your life or someone else's. This right here that happened. It made me get back on the straight street. After this happened to me, I was always asking other people what they thought about other situations. Why? Because I did not trust my own judgment. I was afraid of failure. Because I had failed as a mother by trusting someone else because they were close to me.

All my life, I was controlled by my sister. Whatever she told me, I thought it was the gospel. I have to go this way so that you don't do what I did. I love my sister. She is deceased now. Sometimes, Satan makes you an offer through other people. Especially through someone who is close to you. Remember, I told you that this man worked with my sister. She came back and told me that he said, "Here I am." I bit the bait and took him up on his offer. Even met him at my sister's house. I was just grinning and showing him my legs. And another thing I want to say to you. Some of these men do not care what you look like. You can be well put together. You can show him what you are working with, and he will still mess you up. John 10:10 "The thief commeth not but for to steal, kill and destroy." I come that they might have life and that they might have it more abundantly. We blame God for bad things that happen to us. "Oh, why did this happen to me"? Well, let me help you. In some cases, not all. For example. The warning comes before destruction, and a haughty spirit before a fall. Hebrews 2:1. Sometimes we think we know everything. No one could tell me anything at that time. One day, you are going to listen and hear somebody. If not, it will cost you something over and over. There were a few people who tried to warn me. God loves us so much that he will send out a warning. Stop taking God so lightly. It is hard to hear when Satan has stoppers on both of your ears and blinders on your eyes. Then, after the fact, every little detail comes to you. And you wonder why did I not see that in the midst of it? You are going to have to humble yourself down. We have to learn how to learn from our mistakes. And not keep going over the same ones.

Does it really make sense to keep getting the same type of man? One that never wanted you in the beginning. Sometimes, we think a man who hurt us badly loves us. We will say, "Oh, they had some problems, that's all." Well, the devil is a liar, and the truth is not in him. Don't you believe that. That is a lie from the pits of hell. If a man cannot tell you the truth about himself, especially his past. And if he does not remove himself from you instead of hurting or harming you or someone you love, he does not care about you and never will. You would be a fool to take him back or stay with him. We always think that we can fix a person or their problem. No, we cannot. Only God can help them. I thought keeping this man happy was allowing him to smoke marijuana and drink beer whenever he got his unemployment check. This happened around me and my daughter.

When he did not have these things. A different spirit came over him. You see, now I know what it was. I did not know when I was in the relationship. His face was long and sad, and he was in another world. He would be depressed, and I did not know what to do for him. But when he got his money, he was ok. I would drive him to the dope house to buy weed. What was I thinking? I was getting off track! My umbrella of divine protection was gone. He drove my car and would pick me up from work. I was happy. And the reason I was happy was because I knew he was coming home with me. Do you see how silly we can be? All because we don't want to be alone. We give them keys to our homes, keys to our cars, and keys to our hearts only to be broken. I told you that you will start doing things you have never done in your life. Satan will introduce you to new things. Remember, I said in the beginning that all it takes is one person. One person to change your outer man, and one person to change your enter man, if that be the case. This man introduced me to speed pills. Yellow jackets, Christmas trees. I was not trying to numb the pain of my situation. I somehow just started doing it. Evil communication corrupts good manners. I Corinthians 15:34 and 35. I have to expose myself and be very transparent in order that I may help somebody. I stopped after Janell passed away. This is my real testimony. I started drinking after Janell passed away, and I was all alone. Then I noticed one day when I went to the store to buy a bottle of my favorite drink. I drank the whole bottle, and nothing happened.

I was so disappointed that I didn't get drunk. Don't tell me what God won't do. God delivered me from drinking, speed, and fornication. I can go on and on. I had to learn how to be by myself and wait on God. I am so happy as I give my testimony. Because God is a strong deliverer. Some people tell me that they would have gone crazy if they had gone through losing a child. My God is Awesome. Because he came to set the captive free. This is not the end of my story. I have to tell you when all my troubles began. Abandonment is real. If you don't believe it is real. Ask someone who jumped out of the skillet and into the fire.

My ex-husband was gay. He did not want me. He chose men over me. I saw that the first two years into our marriage. I did not want to believe it or receive it. I was in denial. He lived a double life. One life was in town, and the other life was with me. He would leave me alone, and I sure did not know how to drive. When I did learn to drive. Friends started telling me that they saw him in other places. I did not want to believe until I found out for myself. Put it this way: when he put it in my face and brought it home. He lied to me when we started receiving phone calls at home for him. Then they started showing up at my home, asking for him. Janell was alive then. Some were men in the church, as well as out of the church. I often wondered why guys would look at me funny when we would go out. Some of them were on the down-low. Some of them were married. I started watching him in his attire. One day, pictures that fell out of a case he was dragging through the house spilled out on the floor. I picked them up as he was walking, leaving a trail.

I believe that was one of his ways of telling me. He wanted his cake and eat it too. He told me that some wives don't mind if their husband is gay. Well, I did. You know I still wanted God to heal him, and for us to remain husband and wife. I did not want a divorce. God had to bring me to my senses. I prayed and prayed that he would get delivered. When we separated was when I backslid. I was trying to prove to the world that I was not a failure in my marriage. He would have stayed with me if I would not bother him about it. The funny thing is everybody knew it but me. They all told me after the fact that they knew. I saw things after I married him. Put it this way: I was not sure. The evidence was there. I wish that men who are like that would not marry. I respect the ones that don't marry. That they are honest enough and strong enough not to marry. Knowing that their preference is different. After all, he asked me to marry him. I know you want to ask me if he could perform. Yes, he could. He dressed like a man when we went to church and other places. It got so he was starting to hit and miss. This is where it all started.

I would find different color contact lenses, hidden in the closet. I told you that I could not drive. But others would see him and tell me in their own way. Or their gay brother would tell them where they saw him at gay parties and bars. I wish that the murderer would have told me he was a killer. The detective told me he wanted to tell me. But he was afraid of losing me. My ex-husband told me if he would have been a man, none of this would have happened. I really hope that you, the reader, are being educated through this book of life. Maybe you will never hear me. But please read the book. Both mothers tried to conceal what their sons were. Please tell mothers to tell on these men. If you really love a person, tell them. Don't beat around the bush. Tell me why I should not leave my child with your son. You knew he murdered all those children. Or you see me coming with your son, who is my husband, and you run trying to conceal he is gay.

I was dating a prisoner and was planning on marrying him. I did mention this earlier. His mother loved me enough to tell me that he was suicidal, just like the man who killed my daughter. She told me. I took everything she told me into consideration, along with counseling from my pastor. I did not marry him ever. Take your time. Because if you don't, it will cost you something. Wait on the Lord. Don't get caught up in the celebration or the ring. By the way, my ex-husband stole and sold my wedding ring. He had the nerve to confess it while our daughter lay in a coma at the hospital. "Yeah, I stole them when you put them on the counter." Whenever I would do dishes or mop, I would always lay my wedding rings on the counter. He stole all the income tax money out of the bank when we separated. He knew Janell and I needed the money. From day one he was always stealing from me. My naive and gullible self-did not realize that the thief was right in my face. I slept with him every night. I ate with him every day. I did not know who I was dealing with. The enemy went to the bank with me to get a copy of the hand and the handwriting. It was him. He was doing all this while I was married to him. The killer who murdered Janell. He was sleeping with me and beating my child behind my back.

The reason why I knew this is because the detectives asked me if she had ever gone to a hospital other than when it happened. I told them, No. They never replied back to me. I believe they felt I had been through enough. Be very careful, ladies and gentlemen. This goes for men as well as women. You are looking for a stepmother to put over your children so that you can run the streets. You picked them up for the weekend and got your girlfriend babysitting them. You go to the club or hang out with your boys while leaving your child in the hands of a stranger. That's who they are: Strangers. A stranger is someone you think you know. They are pretending like they just love your child. And immediately, you got them calling her Momma. It's no longer auntie or uncle. You got them calling them Momma or Daddy.

The devil is a liar. You are trying to make your children trust and love them. I had a guy one time who tried to tell me that. That I was his big grown daughter's mother. I told him, no, I am not. I broke that off really quick. Be it man or woman, you do not love your children when you put all these different strangers over your children. You just want a sex partner. Oh yes, I will go there. Someone that you can lay up with and play house and include the child. I know. I did and tried that. And it never worked. Do you think kids don't know? They will remember even when they become adults. That is one of the reasons that they disrespect you. You will reap what you sow. Galatians 6: 7-8 Do not be deceived: God is not mocked, for whatsoever a man soweth that shall he also reap.

And you wonder why they dislike or can't get along with you throughout life. When I came home that day, and found my daughter's dangling body on the knee of this killer, and he was combing her hair. Well, I know now that he was trying to cover up her bruises, concussions, and contusions on her head. I took her into the bedroom, and she said to me, this is what my two-year-old said to me. "He hit!" I then saw the small bruise on her jaw. I hope you are letting all of this sink in. Then he ran on foot to his mother's house. Deceivers are everywhere. Am I trying to scare you straight? Yes, I am. When this happened to my daughter, I said I pray this never happens to anyone else. But as I live on, even after forty-some years, it is still happening. It will continue to happen. We can help, though. We can help by reporting abuse. Please don't ignore that it is still happening. Don't say that he or she looks so kind and loving. And please do not make the excuse that they take to them.

Sometimes, we make them talk to them. When I left for work that morning, Janell was crying. I should have turned around and went back into the house. But instead, I went right to work. This man was full of violence and hate. And the ex-husband was no better. I take full responsibility that I trusted these two men. Know the difference between love and hate. Learn the difference between when someone is covering up something. Or the family is covering up something. A lot of people have hidden agendas. Every day, someone is being tricked or deceived. Some of us are too trustworthy and a little too friendly. And sometimes we are attracted to the wrong people. And we keep getting the same results. Even after some things happen to us, we still haven't woken up yet.

The reason is that we do not wait on God. And we do not acknowledge God in all things. I was a twenty-seven-year-old woman when this happened to me. I regret that I did not keep going. I always had a problem trusting people. I trusted people way too easily. Now, I pray for wisdom and guidance from the Lord. Listen, Satan is trying to destroy us before we can be anything for God. You will never fulfill your purpose in life by latching on to people. Like I said before, we are too trustworthy sometimes. We trust the wrong people. Everyday people are not always right for your situation. Sometimes we think because we see someone else shack or leave their children with someone else. We think we should be able to do it, too. Not So! Your path in life is not like everybody else's. You may not be cut out for this. Everybody's walk is different. "So and so did it, and nothing happened." Jeremiah 29:11 For I know the plans I have for you, declares the Lord. Plans to prosper you and not to harm you. Plans to give you hope and a future. God will not harm you. Don't put all your trust in a man. Jeremiah 17:9: "The heart is deceitful above all things., and desperately wicked; who can know it? I, the Lord, search the heart. I test the mind." Some people have wicked minds. The enemy is always plotting and planning something deceitful for someone's life. There is not a day that goes by that I don't remember what happened to me and Janell on that dreadful day. I hope that you don't think you could ever forget something like that. Please consider what I say!

"Girl, I understand what you are going through. No, you do not. You may feel my pain or their pain, but you really don't know. You can't help them. And you really do wish that you could help them. Only God can. People reached out to me. But I was so stunned and bitter that I could not receive or understand what they meant. I was shocked that it happened to me. "It can happen to you, too." It takes God to replenish and restore us. And sometimes, if we are not careful, we will always be trying to prove to others that we were a good mother or a person. You don't need to prove anything to anybody. That is too much work added on. Sometimes, people are not even looking at you like that. That is your stinking thinking. People have their own problems. And if the truth be told, they have skeletons in their closets, too. And if they know what kind of person that you are, they will not judge you. I don't care how many people tried to help me. I appreciate everyone who reached out to me. But I had to grab hold of God and realize that only he could help me. I have come to know God in a very real way. He is my all and all. And I know I will see Janell again. God is still working on me with trust issues. It is not fair to people who have not ever harmed you to relive what you went through. Some people don't even know it happened to you unless you bring it up to every person you meet.

I remember after Janell died, and a couple of years later someone introduced me to a friend of their husband. He was going to take me to our company Christmas party. I met him at my home. And the first thing I did was start talking about Janell and what happened to her. That guy did not show up to take me to the Christmas party. And I never saw him again. I was not ready. I was still grieving. I was messed up and could have messed someone else up. I kept asking my coworker what happened that he did not come. She just kept saying she did not know. I am, to this day, so glad he did not show up. With the exception of my ex-husband. Everybody else that I met in life, someone always introduced them to me.

I found out later on in life, that is because I had never waited on God. No one has to introduce you to anyone. And just because they seem ok to the person who introduced you. That does not mean that they are going to treat you right. Most men think you are hard up when someone introduces them to you. Now, in some cases, it works, but in some cases it does not. No one knew that man was a killer. It was all speculation. Because each case was under suspension or blunt objects. It was never proven until he confessed to what he did to my baby. Everyone thought he was this quiet guy on the job. I thought so, too until I found out that he was quiet and sneaky. He had everyone fooled. Because he kept getting away with it. Looks can be deceiving. He was very quiet and always grinning around my family. My sister did not know. But someone told her later that they thought he killed other children. And he still got away with it. All because the statute of limitations was ten years. They could not even charge him for their murders. He told a lie each time. The system believed him. He had everyone fooled. So he continued to do it. And I did not believe it when my sister retracted what someone had told her. I never saw anything or heard anything. I was too far gone in my own hurt. These two men had problems that I could not solve. We, as women, have to stop thinking that we can fix a broken man. And we have the nerve to think that we can change them. They will end up changing you in the relationship. And then, when someone else comes along. You treat them bad because you spent and invested all your time and energy on someone who did not even love or care about you. Do not pick someone who is draining the life out of you.

That is why we need to pray for God to take the scales off of our eyes. So that we can see clearly and believe what God is showing us. Oh yes, he does work through other people. You are hearing from God when they try to tell you. God loves us so much that he does not want us to go through all that pain. Then you become suicidal, just like that person told you that he would kill himself if you left them. Please hear me: that type of person will kill or harm you or something you love. That is what happened to me. I would not leave because I thought he needed me and would kill himself. So I stayed there until he took my daughter's life. Little by little, he was abusing my daughter, and little by little I was being inflicted with pain that I would endure later. Even if it is just a rumor, pay attention.

Get out of there as fast as you can. Take your child and run. He can have the apartment. Call the police to get him out. Even if it is just a rumor. Remember that he told me that he would make it, so I never trust a man again. He knew all along what he was going to do. He had already done it three other times. He knew how to hurt me. What a coward. I have had a hard time in my early life trusting men and women. The consequence is that you will not trust anyone ever again. God has to restore that back to you. That trust is broken. Trust God and also trust your gut instincts. This man would sit up and make little matchbox cars all day. I guess that was supposed to keep his mind intact. He told me one time that someone asked him what people think about when they have a nervous breakdown. He said, "Nothing, they don't think about anything. And I still was not getting it. He was telling me that he had some mind problems. In bits and pieces, he was laying out his plan to kill, steal, and destroy. He was dead wrong about me trusting a man again.

He was saying that I would never trust a man again over my child. I have two beautiful children today. A girl almost forty, and a son thirty-nine. God helped me to raise them. I still was a single mother. This time, I never put anyone over these two. A life lesson learned. I waited until they were grown and well on their own before I dated again. Even then, I still had trust issues. You have to let God take you through the process of life. I am honored, happy, and glad to have Jesus Christ in my life. I love him with all that is within me. I will cling to the old rugged cross. If you are going through a divorce and you have children. Sacrifice yourself for your children's well-being. We are to protect our children. I did not protect Janell. Because I was warned to get out of it. Sometimes, God will give you someone who will love and cherish you and your children. I am just saying. Do it the right way. Don't do as I did, trying to find a father for your child. And trying to find a husband for yourself. Who in this world told me and others to take God's place? He did not ask for our help. He said that he would help us in our time of need. Not the need for sex that you miss from being married. Not the need to cover up your loneliness. Not so you can show the world that you were not a failure. Sometimes you get someone worse than what you had. All because you did not wait. You have to stop attracting the wrong spirit of a man. If you are used to men hurting you. Or you always think you can get a humpty dumpty back together again. You are wrong as two left shoes. And you are an accident waiting to happen, along with a lot of mistakes. I want to share this with you also. At the hospital, I was sitting at Janell's bedside in a chair. The two social workers came to visit us that morning. They did not sit down. They just kind of stood there talking to me. They said goodbye and left the room.

Then they walked back in, and one sat on each side of me. Just for a few minutes and did not say anything. They got up and walked out. They wanted to see if I had a fear of men. They wanted to see if I was uncomfortable around them. They wanted to see if I would pull my chair away. Little did they know the aftermath overtook me. Yes, I was very angry, bitter, and hurt. I was very disappointed in myself and also disappointed in what I allowed to happen to my daughter. I say allowed because I was warned. There are some who said they would never leave their boyfriend with their child. You would if you thought that he showed you that he could be trusted. When you are out there in the world, or you backslide as I did. Don't think that the world cannot offer you anything. It has a lot to offer. Understand that we all have a purpose. Even a dog has a purpose to protect or comfort you.

Remember, Satan can appear even while you are praying. And you will think that it is God because it looks like what you prayed for. He even appears as an angel of light. II Corinthians 11:14. We are willing to bargain our very lives and our children's lives to be ruined and damaged for life. The truth of the matter is you may not know that it happened until your children are grown. I do know of incidents where the children did not tell the parents until they were grown. That even some babysitter or some boyfriend or even a natural father did things to them. And you wonder why they are promiscuous. Or why they have a drinking problem. Some don't know whether they are male or female. Not all the time do parents know. You assume they are in good hands. That is the world's way. Believe me, it happens in Christian homes also. I am no better than you, and you are no better than the next person. This could happen to you, too. I don't care how educated you are. It doesn't matter where you went to school. It does not matter if you are rich or poor. It can happen to you, too. It can even happen to a person who works in the professional field.

Stop taking God lightly. Let God take you through some life-changing experience. Where you don't spend your life going through different men thinking he is the right one. Be still. Be anxious for nothing. God is a keeper. You can be kept by his power. I did not know that he could keep me. Because I walked away from him in the midst of my marriage. I was separated when I got this man. I was not divorced. And silly me, I got the divorce so that I would not be sinning, so I thought. He was the one who wanted it. I should have let him get it and pay for it. No big bad me; Satan was ready to jump at the chance to destroy me for life. Because there was purpose in me. You have a purpose, also. Do you know that Satan watches and knows you, too? His purpose is to stop you from being all God wants you to be. We were created for his glory. We are to shine before men so that they may see God's glory in us. You have got to figure this out that you were not made to be trampled on.

Whichever one I choose. The choice still is mine. If I saw you getting ready to cross the street and a car was coming. I saw the car, but you did not. But I did not try to intervene to stop you from crossing the street. So you got hit. And I stood over you saying poor so and so. I knew that car was going to hit you. I could have helped you and stopped you from having a lot of pain that you did not need. You are all broken up, torn into pieces. All because I did not help or warn you. What kind of friend would I be to let you get hurt or killed? Well, I am here today by the grace of God to help and warn you of things that could happen. God uses ordinary people just like me. I come to tell you to heed the warning. Can you imagine the things I have had to go through to be made whole again? Smearing all that bitterness on others. Everybody did not hurt me. I had to first ask God to forgive me. Then, I had to forgive the man who did this to my beautiful daughter. Then, I had to ask Janell while holding her in my arms every day to forgive me. I had to forgive the ex-husband who abandoned Janell and me.

A man who did not love us. A man who came every once in a while to see us. And also seeing what else he could take from us. They both stole from us. The one that took my daughter's life. And the other one came to strip me of everything that I was. What has Satan assigned himself and his demons to take from you? Please hear me. This is for the old and the young, be it men or women. Men get tricked, too. Satan does not have any respect for persons either. So please consider what I say. Choose life. Live to the fullest of God in Christ Jesus. You might say, "Well, I am not saved. Give your heart to Jesus. He is waiting with open arms. Run into his arms and not into a man that could hurt you. A man who could cause you more grief than you can imagine. This man knew that I was trying to leave. He became unemployed. He became a burden to me. It got so I could not stand to be around him, because he had nothing to offer. I stayed too long. I always felt in my heart toward the end that something was terribly wrong. Something just was not right. All the warning signs were there. I was not even his type of woman. We, meaning you and I, have got to stop settling for the worst of what life has to offer. We think that we are not good enough for nobody but the worst. Because that is all you know. The best things in life do not cost you anything. And the strange thing is, we buy into it. I recommend that you find your purpose. God will reveal it to you. You do not have to be like the next person. God made you and I to be original. Don't let no one come along and change you. Grow in the grace of God. Do not be a people pleaser. Just because Satan uses somebody to introduce you to them. It does not mean you have to take them. Tell your friend or your relative no. And please stop looking lonely and desperate. That is when people think it is their job to find you, someone. Stay busy with your children. It does not have to include a man to be with you.

It is God that makes you complete. Colossians 2:10. And you are complete in Him, who is the head of all principality and power. A man does not complete you. We have believed that for so long. Oh, don't let people start judging you because you are by yourself. You have a fit and think you have to go find someone for yourself. So, what if they think you are of the opposite sex? Let them think what they want, too. Check out how they are doing in life. Especially after they have talked about you being alone. I would rather be alone than be with someone who doesn't want me. Or just taking anything that is not for you. Just for the sake of saying you have someone. Not so! God forbid. You do not have to always get rained on. Don't let other people drown you in their sorrow and woes. Let them stay depressed by themselves. You already know that they have problems when they threaten to kill themselves. Do you think that you can fix a person like that?

I don't care how much you give them. I don't care how much they say they love you. Anybody can say that they love you in the midst of a moment of passion. Leave them alone. You can tell them some places to get help for themselves. But most of the time, you will find out later when you are in court and hear everything about them. They had been getting help all alone. You just did not know it. I want you to please listen to me. The man that murdered my daughter. I was going to the hospital to visit him and did not ask what for. I did not ask him why he was in the hospital. I just went. I found out later that he had a nervous breakdown. He admitted himself. He was living right under my roof, and I did not know. I didn't take him to the hospital. He had left me for days, and I did not ask any questions. Listen! The man was taking pills right under my nose. He told me they were for a nervous stomach. I believed him. He would say how the pills coated his tongue. I still did not get it. Every day, he was taking these pills.

In every incident in which this man murdered children, he was not working. His factory job laid him off from time to time. When I met him, he had a job, and it was a good one. As soon as I got him, he got laid off. I was trying to be loyal to him. He started getting unemployment checks. By the way, he had a five-year-old son who would visit us sometimes. He never laid a hand on him. If the truth be told. I don't think he ever stopped seeing the lady that he was previously seeing before me. You see how stupid I was. He was running from her back to me. You understand that all this has come together and made sense to me later.

I was young and did not know anything but marriage. That was horrible enough. This book that God has inspired me to write. You are too good of a person to just keep settling. For what reason are we so desperate to have someone? That we would take just anything. Sometimes, we don't care what they look like. We just want a man. Sometimes, we don't even know if he is a man. Isaiah 4:1 says, on that day seven women will take hold of one man and say, we will eat our own food and provide our own clothes, only let us be called by your name. To take away our disgrace.

Let me read this in the King James version. Isaiah 4:1 And in that day seven women shall take hold of one man, saying we will eat our own bread. And wear our own apparel. Only let us be called by thy own name. Does that make sense to you? Because it is happening right now in this day and age. We women want to do it all. All because we settle. Every man is not the same. There are some men who want to take care of you. We will do anything just to have his last name. I don't care how many bad men there are. There are still some good men in this world. What an insult to God if you think there is not. They are looking for good women like you and I. They cannot find us because we are hidden behind the wrong things. We need to let God work on us. Some of us have been through a lot of stuff. We have been wounded so badly until we have stopped loving ourselves first. Taking care of yourself is essential. I am not talking about only the natural man. I am talking about that person who needs their heart repaired. How about allowing God to work on our attitudes? So we don't carry the old man into a new relationship.

Please don't take a man who is not ready. You see him and want him. And you accept him as is. A lot of times, we buy cars as is. Because we are used to buying the same car with problems. I know we have to start somewhere. And we usually get what we can afford. Don't you want something better? We get what we think we can afford. Sometimes God has elevated our minds to not look back. Sometimes, he has brought you out of poverty, and we are still staying there. Have you ever seen a dog that has been chained up for so long that when his master turns him loose, he does not realize he is free? He is still lying or sitting there. He has not realized that he is free. We live sometimes like we are still in bondage. When God has sat everything before us on his table. Don't you want the man to come from God? Then, do something different and wait on God. A lady told me one time who was a back slider. We used to go to church together. She looked at me and said, "I miss the world." She said, "I miss some of the things I did in the world." There is something wrong when you don't want anything better. Especially after you have tasted the goodness of God, the devil will fool you and make you think you are missing something.

You go back out there! You may not make it back into the body of Christ. You are taking a grave chance. I had a lot of people that were praying for me. They would come in the hospital room. And they would pray and leave. Sometimes, they said nothing to me. They just would pray. The reason why I love the Lord so much. He really heard my cry. And He brought me up out of a horrible pit. No one knew how I really felt after Janell's death. They thought I was being so strong. God was holding me all the time. Sometimes, it could be eighty or ninety degrees outside. I would be riding home from work with no air on with my windows rolled up. I could not stand for the doors to the bathroom to be shut. I would use the public restroom without locking the stall door. I was trapped in my own mind. All because I was trapped in a relationship that was not meant to be.

I thought about getting my daughter and running out of it. But I didn't do it. I felt like I was frozen and could not move. I felt like something was going to happen to me. I never thought that it was happening to my daughter. Before Janell passed away, it was my sister who would take her to church on Sundays. I would be stuck at home with the man. I had completely stopped going to church. His mother was a Jehovah's Witness. She told me I would have to become one in order to get married to her son. So I did go a few times, Janell and I with him. He had murdered two children and disabled one child and was going to church. I knew better. Because that was not the way I was brought up in my faith. He had already murdered a little girl, and I allowed him to be over mine. In his mother's eyes, he was ok. Not only in his mother's eyes, but in the whole family that came to Indiana with them.

I found out later that some terrible things had happened in that family among themselves. They were kept secret among them. Get a background check. Ask someone who knows them. And the information that they give you. Take it and run. Don't do it like I did and take it lightly. Not only get a background check, but you make sure to check them out, too. Use the five senses that God has given us. Stop being so needy when God has everything you need. Concentrate on the children and yourself so that they can have a bright future. It is not about you. Don't let the devil fool you. He will present a fake imitation of what you are supposed to have. Please stop getting attracted to the same type of man. It will never work. Taking from you all the time is their gain. You get nothing in return but failure and misery.

If you allow this to happen to you. Unless you let God work in the midst, you will never let anyone get close to you again. You will need help to gain trust again from everybody. You will find it hard to connect with other people. You will find yourself backing out of some wonderful things that God has for you. You will miss opportunities that were meant for you. All because you did not wait. I know this to be true. Because if I would have taken my life like I planned it. I would not be telling my story to help other young women and men. God has given me a wonderful life. More than I can imagine. And because He lives, I can face tomorrow. And for the rest of my life, I will serve the Lord. I am strong in the Lord. I depend on him for everything. I had to learn life lessons. They have taught me a lot. It is ok to be alone. I am not alone because I have Jesus in my life. One of my relatives told me when I got a divorce that Janell and I did not look right alone. They told me to go and get myself a man. So I did what they said. And after everything happened, they talked bad about me. Don't listen to people. The ones that had a bad life themselves.

Some people can see if you are weak and gullible. And they will play on that. I have learned to step away from those kinds of people. I go to God in prayer, and I talk to him all the time. Stay in the word of God. I really am not concerned about how I may look to other people. I am not going to go out and get something to make me look good. In my opinion, I stay away from people who always want to talk about having a man. I am still waiting, and they are remarried and got a divorce. They ran to me to dangle their rings in my face. Now, they are divorced again and bitter. Some only stayed married for a couple of years, and their spouse passed away. Now, they are alone again, hurt and angry at the world. Wait, I say on the LORD. God will give you double for your trouble.

I am reminded of Hannah in the book of Samuel and how she was a barren woman and could bear no children. In Samuel 1:1-20, Elkanah was the husband of two wives. One could bear children, and the other could not. Peninnah. The other wife could have children. Hannah wept and cried out to God. She promised God that if he gave her a man-child, she would give him back. God opened up her womb, and she gave birth and called him Samuel. She weaned him and gave him back to God. Now, what are you going to do when God bless you and me with a man of God? Are you going to still serve God? I want you to know many counterfeits are going to come before the real blessing. The distractions will come to try to detour you from God. You can be working in ministry or on God's purpose for what he has for you. And here comes a distraction. You can be saying, "I am really going to stay on track this time. But your adversary, the devil, seeking whom he may devour, is also on your track to make you forget about your God-given purpose in life. And every time you start making progress, here comes a man. You start running from the gift and begin chasing the man. What happened to the dream God gave you?

I myself was working on music. I am a songwriter, and I also record gospel music. Every time a man would come, I would lay the music down. I hope you are listening to what I am saying. Satan's aim is to stop you. That you may never become what God has called you to be. We even have the audacity to ask God if he can send a man or a husband to help us. And sometimes he does that. But some of us will never become what God has ordained us to be if we get someone beforehand. God knows who will and who won't.

We can never fool the almighty God. He will let us have it sometimes so that we can see where we are. You will also have to minister to your husband. You will have to please him. You are out of order if you don't. There are some who wish they never would have gotten married. Because now you feel like the man is in the way. When I refer to men, I am also talking to men or women. So be careful of what you try to make happen in your life on your own. Stay focused. I myself am still waiting on some things from God. One of the biggest blessings that I have in life. I am learning to wait on God and trust in his promises. Now, if you know that God has promised you some things in life. Maybe you asked him for it. And you may feel that he promised it to you. Stay in his will and never try to make it happen. Watch out for following different church meetings when you hear of someone coming to your city. And you want to hear a word concerning your situation! Be very careful. There is nothing wrong with a confirmation; just be careful. You will start imagining in your mind and visualizing him next to you. The next thing you will try to do is put it into action. The first person that comes along, you will think that is it. You will think because you prayed, God sent it right then and right away. All God ever told me to do was to wait.

I do know of many situations where people are in high places. I know of people that believed and received the word, whatever it was. They were tricked. For instance, I can talk about myself. I was invited to a prayer meeting one time. The lady was of such high standards that I trusted her judgment. She was praying over me and said that she saw a man attached to me on my side in the spirit. I just could not receive that from her. I was puzzled. She later came back and corrected herself. She told me later that it was not from God but from what she thought she had seen. I John 4:1-5. Beloved believe not every spirit, but try the spirits whether they are of God because many false prophets are gone out into the world. It did not line up with the word of God. Isn't it wonderful how God wants to protect us from harm and danger? Or even making a complete fool of ourselves.

"God told me you were my mate. Well, I got news for you. He has to tell me, too. I was dating a man one time. Some of the things I saw him do, I knew it was not from God. He was a smoker, a fornicator, and other things that God had already delivered me from. I said to myself this is not sent from God. All I could think of was all the time I waited for God, and I was getting This! The devil is a liar, and the truth is not in him. He knew some word or some kind of word. Other people knew him, and I did not. The things that he said he was delivered from, he was still doing. That would have pulled me back into the world. I let it go. When I was in the world, he still was not my type of man. Am I helping somebody? Listen, we all make mistakes. So don't beat yourself down if you have done such a thing. You were tricked and deceived. "Get up from there and ask God to clean you up. Don't think just because you did it, you are to stay there. You see, that is where we mess up. We feel that I am in it now. I might as well stay. No, No, No. God will restore you.

The devil likes it when you feel equal to the person that you messed up with. That was his plan all along. He wants to kill you and hurt you. So you can wonder how in the world did I get here. Christians fall, and people fall. You can get up from there and declare to the devil, "I am coming out." Tell the devil he is a defeated foe. That way, you will be a winner. You are stronger than what you think. If you feel that you are in a way and you cannot get out. Ask God to help you. You will never stay out of it doing it on your own. Remember, many times, I promised God that I would leave this man alone, who murdered my daughter. I made a promise to God and did not keep it. You have found out through reading my book what happened, the end results.

When God keeps sending you a warning. If you refuse to take heed to it. Over and over, you play with fire. Sooner or later, you are going to get burned. Why? Because the enemy's job is to consume you. What can be worse than someone killing your first-born child whom you just adore? The devil knows that you adore them, too. No mother or father wants to bury their children. You don't want to look down upon them in a tiny casket. Something that could have been prevented. If you would just have listened to somebody. If you would have just kept going and not looked back. If you would not have kept saying yes to satan. Even after the matter, you still were trying to make it happen. I want a husband is all that is in your head. You can't keep the bird from flying over your head. But you can stop him from making a nest in your head. The thoughts may come. Pray and do not do what your flesh wants to do. You have to override and diminish those kinds of thoughts. You have to move on. There are better fish to catch. You have dreams. You can let God work on your attitude; God has given you brand new beginnings. Then you will not have to look over so many regrets. You don't want a life full of regrets. There is not a minute that goes by that I am not thinking of my Nell Nell. Wishing that she was here to enjoy life with me and my other two children.

I hope that I am still helping you. Will you consider what I say? Haven't you been hurt enough in life? Consider that someone is pouring into you everything that there is that would cause you to look in the mirror and see how beautiful you are. To understand that God made you who you are and what you are. This beautiful plan that he has put together and handpicked Himself. One that would cause you to think you are the only one he did it for. Of course God tells us in his word, whosoever will let him come. I could not close this book without an invitation to sit at Jesus' feet and be blessed. I was a broken vessel that needed to be guided by God's Holy Spirit and presence. I was once blind, and now I see as I walk into the ark of the safety of Jesus Christ. There is no better place to be.

I am kept by his power. I am not a desperate woman anymore, looking for other desperate people to fulfill my needs. I am not trying to make myself feel or look important or trying to prove anything because of what happened to me. God has proved himself in me. And he will prove himself in you also. Will you give God a chance to love you the way you are supposed to be loved? And you sure do not need to be validated by anyone. Some of us are trying to please other people so that they can tell us who we are. It will cost you nothing, Not even getting into a prayer line for someone to tell you who you are. You are a different breed, and you belong to the king. I'm just a little evangelist and missionary who tries with the help of God. To spread the good news that Jesus heals. It does not matter how long you have been in a situation where you are being controlled by the enemy. You can be delivered from that seducing spirit. You know, the one that pulls you by the nose and guides you around. When you don't know how in the world you got there.

And when satan is done dragging you around and is finished with you. He goes to the next person. You did not like being dragged around at first. Being made to do what he wants you to do. You are no match for satan. It takes the grace of God to get you out of your mess. It also will take a miracle because he aims to kill you so that you will never get back to God. I am talking to the backslider now. When Satan was done with me, I was very empty. Low self-esteem. Drained of everything I ever was. Thinking that I did not deserve anything better. Letting people treat me in any kind of way. All because of what I went through. You and I deserve everything that God had for us in the beginning. You will begin to say, "Now, I see Lord. I once was blind, but now I see."

Stop being jealous because you got caught, and they did not. You were chosen. You thought you could rule your own world. We are nothing without God. Can I get an Amen? You are not the boss. You have to learn how to submit to God first. How are you going to be submissive to a husband? Because of all the abuse and pain that you have been through in your life. You have not been healed. God sent his word to heal us. You want to beat up the next man that hurt you. You want to kill all the men for one man that hurt you. Don't let a man look at you like he wants to get to know you. You got your back with a hump in it, like a raging cat. That's how I was. "Don't say anything to me because I am mad." No one is ever going to hurt me again. Do you really believe that you will never be hurt again? Well, I got news that you can use. In this life, you will be hurt. Some of us are so emotional and timid that everything bothers and hurts us. Even if something happens to you, even the most terrible thing. You are going to hurt again. God has sent his word to heal us. Psalms 104:20. He sent his word, and healed them, and delivered them from their destructions. Only God can deliver you. People thought I was doing ok. I wanted to die. But the power of God kept holding me up. I do not have those intentions anymore. Now, if I feel a certain way, I know to go to God in prayer. I am somebody in God. And you are, too.

Yes, he is a sin-forgiving Savior. Nobody can do you like God can what the devil meant for evil. God turned it into good. He planned to take me out. But God, in all of his awesome power, snatched me out of the clutches of sin. He wanted me to see that he was all I needed in life. Anything else is the favor of God. Life is worth living because he lives. That is why I can face each and every day. Jesus took care of everything on the cross at Calvary. All you and I need to do is to die to sin. The guilt and shame are all gone. He took care of that, too. Romans 13:8-10 "Owe no man anything but to love." I owe Jesus my life. A life that is pleasing to him. People make mistakes in life. You don't need to wallow in sin when you can be forgiven. You can move on in life. It happened. God brought you through it.

God did that for you, and I. Christ did it all. Jesus has already bared the cross. Why are you still carrying it? Are you trying to pick up where Jesus has done, done everything that needs to be done? There is nothing left for you to do! You can start living a life that is pleasing unto God. Repent first of all. Some people ask me why am I still single. I am not afraid of a commitment. I am hidden in God. I have to do things the way that's the way of God. You see, my old way was to try to make things happen on my own. Well, I tried all of that, and it did not work for me.

You are looking over the fence at someone else and how they did it. I have had every kind of thing in my life. Now, I want to know how that is working for you. My mother used to say, "A heap sees, but a few know. You don't know what another person had to go through in order to get to where they are today. And things can look so sweet and peaceful. So wait your turn. It's coming. We sometimes always try to jump up there. We do not want to wait. Microwave it, please! Hurry up, Hurry up. I want it right now. Give it to me before I get too old.

Give it to me before my hair turns gray and falls out. Give it to me before I start to get restless. Give it to me while my nerves are still good. Give it to me while I am still young and pretty. Give it to me while I am still healthy.

You will never be good enough with that type of mindset God knows what is in us. He knows what needs to go in us or come out of us. We don't always know what is best for us. That is why we have to depend on God. He made us and he knows all about us. We don't want to accept the fact that we may not get picked. It is a scary thing to think that you may be alone.

We are never alone. You can be married and still feel alone. "Just let me have your last name. You want to settle for less. You want to hold on to that last name for the sake of saying you are still married. Wait on God. I am not telling you to get a divorce, even in the midst of wanting a divorce. You still need to wait instead of doing like I did while I was separated. Wanting to hurry up and make it legal. You are not giving yourself space to see what you really want. Especially when children are involved, whether, they don't want you or not, don't make a drastic decision just because they did. Are you listening? Do you hear me? That way, you pay for the divorce, and you also may pay later for making mistakes that could have been prevented. Didn't you hear me say I took the killer and was not divorced from my ex-husband?

I started letting him live with me. He had nothing. He had gotten laid off from his job. He had nothing. And he made sure that he stayed up under me. I could not keep him there at first. He wanted a place to live. He and his previous girlfriend had broken up. When he lost his job, she dumped him, and I picked up where she left off. He never touched her two girls. He had a job the entire time that he was with her. Then I got him, and he had nothing. I hope that you can see how Satan can so easily trick you. I went from a gay man to a murderer? How could this happen to me? By moving too fast and not paying attention. We need to take our time in life. Along with my divorce, I went back to my maiden name. Not thinking about that, I still had a daughter with his last name. I was very selfish, thinking about no one but myself. And also how to be vengeful.

What did that do? I had a beautiful wedding. A husband whom I loved, and a beautiful baby girl. Who could ask for more. Until I began to see the dark side of my marriage. It only takes one person, or one bad apple to spoil the whole bunch.

Who would not love for someone to come along and ask you to marry them? Just be careful. Sometimes, the signs are all there. We get so blinded by love and don't see it always change after you marry them. No, it was there all the time, Satan does not want you to see the whole picture. Oh, by the way, his best man, who was his best friend, was also gay. This is real talk. Am I still helping you? He came around our home every day. Until our baby girl was born, he started to distance himself. I often used to wonder why he never took to our daughter. His father never came to our wedding. And he would never allow me to talk to his father. All the signs were there. His father asked me after the death of our daughter if they were dating.

I told you that a heap sees, but a few know. And if it walks like a duck and it quacks like a duck. Guess what? It is no doubt a duck. Seeing is believing. Don't pretend you did not see what you saw. You see it. It is a matter of receiving what you see and don't take God for granted. "I need to see more, we say". How much more do you need to see or hear? The one man showed me who he was. The other man told me who he was. What more do you need? What kind of information are you still looking for to convince you of the truth? Getting married under false pretense and knowing that you desire something else is false. But you live in silence until you get tired of being made a fool of. Wake up! Or you will be shaken up by the truth and harrow that will deceive you.

Before all of this happened, I had a good babysitter who was trustworthy, an older woman in her eighties, I believe. She was very good to my daughter. And for no reason at all. I took her out of her care. I put her in harm's way after the fact that I was warned. You can be black, white, tall, short, educated, and smart. And still do dumb things that you will regret later. I don't claim to be innocent in all of this. I should have waited and not been so trustworthy. The last thing I would like to share with you is that you are trying to get even with the person who hurt you in the beginning. You are going to go through more pain and suffering in your entire life. You never have to be vengeful. You continue to serve God as you were.

Do all you can to keep your children and yourself safe from harm and danger? If you are not a born-again Christian. This goes for you to receive Jesus Christ as your lord and Savior. Don't wait until tragedy happens.

Does tragedy always have to happen to you to come to your senses? Some things can be prevented in life. Lighting doesn't always have to strike you.

Will you take heed today?

Will you consider that it can happen to you, too?

Amen and Amen